LIGHTNING BOLT BOOKS™

T0005279

Japanese Spider Crabs

Nature's Biggest Arthropod

Walt Brody

Lerner Publications • Minneapolis

Lerner Publications Company
An imprint of Lerner Publishing Group, Inc.
241 First Avenue North
Minneapolis, MN 55401 USA

For reading levels and more information, look up this title at www.lernerbooks.com.

Main body text set in Billy Infant Regular. Typeface provided by SparkType.

Editor: Annie Zheng **Photo Editor:** Annie Zheng

Library of Congress Cataloging-in-Publication Data

Names: Brody, Walt, 1978- author.
Title: Japanese spider crabs : nature's biggest arthropod / Walt Brody.
Description: Minneapolis : Lerner Publications, [2024] | Series: Lightning bolt books. Nature's most massive animals | Includes bibliographical references and index. | Audience: Ages 6-9 | Audience: Grades 2-3 | Summary: "Do you know what the world's largest arthropod is? It's the Japanese spider crab! Emerging readers will love learning more about the ocean's gentle giants, including what they eat and how they grow"— Provided by publisher.
Identifiers: LCCN 2023003668 (print) | LCCN 2023003669 (ebook) | ISBN 9798765608425 (library binding) | ISBN 9798765615423 (epub)
Subjects: LCSH: Spider crabs—Juvenile literature. | Crabs—Juvenile literature. | BISAC: JUVENILE NONFICTION / Animals / Marine Life
Classification: LCC QL444.M33 B77 2024 (print) | LCC QL444.M33 (ebook) | DDC 595.3/86—dc23/eng/20230206

LC record available at https://lccn.loc.gov/2023003668
LC ebook record available at https://lccn.loc.gov/2023003669

Manufactured in the United States of America
1-1009287-51496-4/11/2023

Table of Contents

Meet the Japanese Spider Crab

A Japanese spider crab crawls slowly along the ocean floor. It has ten legs. Each leg can be up to 5 feet (1.5 m) long.

A hard shell called a carapace protects a Japanese spider crab.

Japanese spider crabs are the world's largest arthropod. Arthropods are animals that have skeletons on the outside of their bodies.

Japanese Spider Crab Eggs

A female Japanese spider crab lays up to 1.5 million eggs per season. The mother does not take care of the eggs after she lays them.

Larvae grow and become adult Japanese spider crabs.

The eggs hatch after about ten days. Then they are called larvae. The larvae are very small and have round, legless bodies.

As the larvae grow, their round bodies change shape. They start growing legs. Their eyes begin to form.

Japanese spider crab eye

A small Japanese spider crab crawls behind a larger Japanese spider crab.

The crabs molt, or shed their outer shell, several times as they grow. Every time they molt, they look more like adult Japanese spider crabs.

At Home at the Bottom

Japanese spider crabs live off the coast of Japan in the Pacific Ocean. They live in deep waters up to 1,800 feet (550 m) below the surface.

Japanese spider crabs are scavengers. These crabs move slowly, so they eat things such as dead sea creatures and plants.

A Japanese spider crab crawls along the bottom of a bay in Japan.

Japanese fishers pulling a fishing net

People fish for Japanese spider crabs in Japan. Since the crabs live in deep waters, people catch them using small nets.

Octopuses, stingrays, and large fish also hunt Japanese spider crabs. The crabs have long arms and large claws to defend against predators.

Octopuses are one of the Japanese spider crab's main predators.

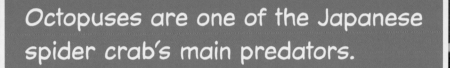

A Japanese Spider Crab's Life Cycle

Japanese spider crabs mate between January and April. They move to shallower waters to mate.

A female Japanese spider crab's belly

After mating, the female carries the eggs. The eggs are attached to the female's belly. Once she lays the eggs, they hatch and grow quickly.

A scuba diver holds up a Japanese spider crab at an aquarium in Tokyo, Japan.

Japanese spider crabs' legs never stop growing. Some crabs can grow up to 12.5 feet (3.8 m) long from claw to claw!

These crabs tend to live alone. They usually forage for food by themselves.

A lone Japanese spider crab

Tasmanian giant crab

Japanese spider crabs are not the only giant crabs. The Tasmanian giant crab's carapace can grow up to 18 inches (46 cm) wide. Its carapace is bigger than the Japanese spider crab's.

The Tasmanian giant crab may have a bigger carapace, but the Japanese spider crab is bigger overall. Its size and claws can make it look fierce, but it is known as a gentle giant of the ocean.

Japanese spider crabs can live up to one hundred years in the sea.

Japanese Spider Crab Diagram

eye

carapace

claw

mouth

leg

Fun Facts

- In Japan, people eat Japanese spider crabs.

- If a Japanese spider crab loses a leg, it grows back.

- Japanese spider crabs are the world's longest arthropod. The American lobster is the world's heaviest arthropod. The heaviest recorded lobster was 44 pounds (20 kg).

Glossary

arthropod: animals without backbones that have segmented bodies, jointed limbs, and skeletons on the outside of their bodies

carapace: the shell around a crab's main body

forage: to look for food

larva: an early stage of a crab's life

mate: when animals breed

molt: to shed hair, feathers, outer shells, or other parts

predator: an animal that hunts and eats other animals

scavenger: an animal that feeds on dead animals and plants

Learn More

Bassier, Emma. *Japanese Spider Crabs*. North Mankato, MN: DiscoverRoo, 2020.

Fact Animal: Japanese Spider Crab Facts
https://factanimal.com/japanese-spider-crab/

Fenmore, Taylor. *Blue Whales: Nature's Biggest Mammal.* Minneapolis: Lerner Publications, 2024.

Harris, Bizzy. *Crabs*. Minneapolis: Pogo, 2022.

Kiddle: Arthropod Facts for Kids
https://kids.kiddle.co/Arthropod

Monterey Bay Aquarium: Japanese Spider Crab
https://www.montereybayaquarium.org/animals/animals-a-to-z/japanese-spider-crab

Index

Photo Acknowledgments

Image credits: slowmotiongli/iStock/Getty Images, p. 4; kateafter/iStock/Getty Images, p. 5; Bigc Studio/Shutterstock, pp. 6, 7; dokosola/Shutterstock, p. 8; Robert Schaub/flickr, p. 9; Norikazu/Shutterstock, p. 10; Ken Usami/Photodisc/Getty Images, pp. 11, 20; DoublePHOTO studio/Shutterstock, p. 12; A. Martin UW Photography/Moment/Getty Images, p. 13; BERENGERE CAVALIER/Alamy Stock Photo, p. 14; MilanMarkovic78/Shutterstock, p. 15; Jeff Rotman/Alamy Stock Photo, p. 16; Jane Rix/Shutterstock, p. 17; Southern Lightscapes-Australia/Moment/Getty Images, p. 18; pr2is/iStock/Getty Images, p. 19.

Cover: Urs Flueeler/EyeEm/Getty Images.